She
Persisted

··

WANGARI MAATHAI

··

—INSPIRED BY—

She Persisted

by Chelsea Clinton & Alexandra Boiger

WANGARI MAATHAI

Written by
Eucabeth Odhiambo

Interior illustrations by
Gillian Flint

PHILOMEL

↝ *This book is dedicated* ↜
to my mother, whose commitment,
kindness, and community involvement
reminds me of Wangari.

PHILOMEL BOOKS
An imprint of Penguin Random House LLC, New York

First published in the United States of America by Philomel Books, an imprint of Penguin
Random House LLC, 2022

Text copyright © 2022 by Chelsea Clinton
Illustrations copyright © 2022 by Alexandra Boiger

Philomel Books is a registered trademark of Penguin Random House LLC.

Visit us online at penguinrandomhouse.com.

Library of Congress Cataloging-in-Publication Data is available.

Printed in the United States of America

HC ISBN 9780593353561
10 9 8 7 6 5 4 3 2 1
PB ISBN 9780593353585
10 9 8 7 6 5 4 3 2 1

WOR

Edited by Jill Santopolo and Talia Benamy.
Design by Ellice M. Lee.
Text set in LTC Kennerley.

Dear Reader,

As Sally Ride and Marian Wright Edelman both powerfully said, "You can't be what you can't see." When Sally said that, she meant that it was hard to dream of being an astronaut, like she was, or a doctor or an athlete or anything at all if you didn't see someone like you who already had lived that dream. She especially was talking about seeing women in jobs that historically were held by men.

I wrote the first *She Persisted* and the books that came after it because I wanted young girls—and children of all genders—to see women who worked hard to live their dreams. And I wanted all of us to see examples of persistence in the face of different challenges to help inspire us in our own lives.

I'm so thrilled now to partner with a sisterhood of writers to bring longer, more in-depth versions of these stories of women's persistence and achievement to readers. I hope you enjoy these chapter books as much as I do and find them inspiring and empowering.

And remember: If anyone ever tells you no, if anyone ever says your voice isn't important or your dreams are too big, remember these women. They persisted and so should you.

Warmly,
Chelsea Clinton

She
Persisted

WANGARI MAATHAI

TABLE OF CONTENTS

. . . .

Born to the Land

When Mount Kenya's snow-capped peak was covered with a blanket of clouds, the people knew the rains were coming. The rains that filled the rivers and streams. The rains that gave life. One very special life came into being during that season. Wangari Maathai was born on April 1, 1940, during the rainy period. Her childhood was woven through with the flowing rivers and streams, and the animals and people of her bountiful country.

As soon as Wangari was born, everyone sprang into action! The women formed a circle of loving care around mother and baby. They made a nourishing meal from the choicest vegetables in their gardens. Even before offering her baby milk, Wangari's mother chewed small bites of

roasted bananas, sugarcane, and sweet potatoes into a smooth juice. She put the juice into her baby's tiny mouth, sharing the strength of the land and their community.

Wangari was born in a small village in Kenya called Nyeri, a part of the country with lush green shrubs, ferns, and trees. There the rain fell on the nearby fields of blue-purple sugarcane, on the forested hillsides where animals like elephants, leopards, antelopes, and monkeys made their home, and on the grass-thatched roof of the separate hut where Wangari's father prepared another feast to celebrate the birth of their first daughter. The same rain that caused everything to grow seemed to welcome baby Wangari into her new world. That same rain would help provide food for her to grow like a strong tree, and bringing back the trees would be her reason to fight to heal the land.

Wangari's parents, Muta Njugi and Wanjiru Kibicho, were Kikuyu people. Life for the Kikuyu revolved around nature. They believed that Mount Kenya, also known as Kirinyaga or "Place of Brightness," was a sacred place. They believed that God, Ngai, lived there and provided everything they needed: the land, the rain, the plants, and the animals. As long as the mountain stood strong and steadfast, they believed that God was with them.

Little Wangari toddled after her two older brothers and her mother, imitating everything she saw. Like most African girls at the time, Wangari learned from her mother. Known as Lydia, she sewed clothes for her family and gardened. Wangari would watch as she, with the help of woman

relatives and friends, regularly roofed their grass-thatched hut.

When Wangari was growing up, Kenya was under the control of the United Kingdom. Life was hard because of the British colonists. The British didn't respect the land and traditions and imposed their own way of life on the people. People in Kenya suffered as a result. The British colonizers cut down trees to clear huge fields for farming, brought in different types of plants that ruined the soil, and hunted the animals that shared the land. The Kenyan people had to follow the laws of the landowners who now ruled them.

Instead of having small farms that grew just enough for each family, many people were displaced and had to work on large plantations run by British colonizers; others needed to work to pay the taxes introduced by the British government. Christian missionaries tried to change the beliefs of the people, preaching that God did not dwell on Mount Kenya but rather in heaven.

When Wangari was very young, her father left the village to work on a plantation in Nakuru, one hundred miles away. Not too long after that, Wangari and her mother left the forested hillside where she had been born and followed him to a vast flat valley planted with field after field of wheat and maize. When they left Nyeri, Wangari left behind everything she knew. But she was too young to worry about what it would be like where she was going. She felt safe because her mother was with her.

. . . .

CHAPTER 2

Glorified Slaves

Wangari was three years old when she got to Nakuru, and there she joined in the flow of life like all her other siblings. She was eager to help as best she could. She cared for her two younger sisters, Muringi and Wachatha, while her mother planted wheat and maize, plucked weeds, and harvested crops in Mr. Neylan's fields. As she got older, Wangari also did household chores and ran errands, like fetching their family's daily ration of maize flour and a liter (a little more than a quart) of milk that was their payment for the day's work.

Wangari and her family, along with others, lived as tenants (called "squatters") on Mr. Neylan's farm. They were required to work in exchange for flour and milk. They never went hungry, but they lived like "glorified slaves." That means that they were treated harshly, like enslaved people were, but they could leave if they wanted to. Many people did not leave, though, because their land had been taken by the British and they had nowhere else to go.

There were no schools for squatter children at Mr. Neylan's farm, or even nearby. Wangari stayed busy helping support the family. While taking care of her sisters, she would cast her eyes to the fields around her, where older children picked beautiful pyrethrum flowers used for making insecticide, which was an insect-killing spray. Wangari dreamed of joining them because it looked like a pleasant job.

Wangari loved the open fields where she felt free to enjoy nature. She would gaze at the endless fields of wheat, watching and listening as the wind made waves through the knee-high grasses. After maize harvest, she and her siblings grazed their goats and sheep in the freshly cut fields and feasted on the small, yellow, juicy managu berries. She would eat so much that she would be too full to eat supper, when her family would enjoy the leaves of the managu vegetable as their meal.

One day her father called her. It was not a common thing for him to call her. She wondered what he had to say.

"You are going to Nyeri so you can help your mother take care of your younger sister," he told her.

So Wangari, her mother, and one of her younger sisters returned to Nyeri, where her two brothers had been living in the care of their uncle Kamunya so that they could attend school. Her other younger sister joined a bit later as well. Wangari was happy to go back to Nyeri as long as she was with her mother.

Nyeri was even more beautiful than Wangari remembered, full of all shades of green. Vegetation covered the fertile brown soil. The snow-capped Mount Kenya seemed to stand guard to the north, and there were even more mountains to the west. Green valleys dotted with bananas, yam, arrow-roots, and sugarcane gardens spread before her. She took a deep breath, drawing in the fresh highland air. She was back home.

Wangari had many things to relearn. For example, at eight, having spent five years in flat Nakuru, she did not know how to go down a steep hillside. She watched her cousins and brothers run down the hill. At first, thinking she would fall, she crawled down the hill backward. But before long, Wangari was mud-skiing just like her cousins. The children were encouraged to play in the rain and hailstorms because it was believed that the rain would make them grow the way it made plants grow. Wangari wanted to grow as tall as a tree.

As she grew up, Wangari continued to do chores just like her mother and the other women in the village did. She would go into the wood lot behind her house, collect fallen firewood, and carry the bunch on her back while singing. On arriving home, she would throw off the wood and sit on it, just like she had seen her mother and the other women do.

Trees had great meaning for Wangari. She knew that they were important for life, and that she needed to take care of all things that nature provided and respect them. Whenever she was sent to collect firewood, she made sure not to touch the migumo, or fig, trees.

Her mother would remind her, "Don't pick any dry wood out of the fig tree, or even around it."

"Why?" Wangari would ask.

"Because that's a tree of God," her mother would reply. "We don't use it. We don't cut it. We don't burn it."

Wangari would approach the migumo tree almost reverently and drink the fresh sparkling water from the Kanungu stream nearby. She would sit quietly watching where the stream bubbled out of the earth. There she played with frog eggs, gently picking up the bead-like eggs and trying to place them around her neck, but they would slip right out of her hands back into the water. Soon she would hear frogs croaking around the river. Later she would understand the connection between the tadpoles and the frogs, the clear water and the trees, the mountains and the rain.

Wangari enjoyed hiding under the large elephant ear–like leaves of the arrowroot plants when it rained. Out in the forest, Wangari listened to birds and learned their names. One day, Wangari's mother gave her a small garden of her own. Her mother knew that Wangari would learn more that way than by simply helping in her mother's garden. She taught Wangari how to plant and care for crops by herself. She would remind Wangari to plant during the rain. One time, Wangari got bored watching her plants grow, so she lifted the seeds out of the ground to see how quickly they were growing.

"No, no, no," her mother said. "You don't remove them. You have to cover them. You have to let them do all this by themselves. Soon they will all come above the ground." With her mother's help, Wangari learned a great deal about planting and letting plants grow.

She did not know that one day many of the birds, animals, and trees would be gone, yet a love for nature was planted in her heart as she worked

and played. This love would give her the confidence to speak out and fight for these hills, forests,
streams, and living creatures later on.

....

CHAPTER 3

Growing Minds Like Trees

In Nyeri, Wangari continued to help her mother with house chores while the boys went to school. At that time, most girls in the village didn't attend school. Her brother Nderitu had other ideas. He wanted Wangari to attend school, too, and their mother agreed. There were just a few girls in school, and Wangari was determined to learn as much as possible. It wasn't easy. At eight years old, she walked three miles to school every day. The classroom was freezing cold during part of the year. Furthermore, they had to bring ashes and water to clean the mud floor. Even in such conditions, though, Wangari excelled.

When she was eleven years old, she entered St. Cecilia Intermediate Primary School, a boarding school in Nyeri. At St. Cecilia, she was taught by nuns of the Catholic church. Wangari worked hard and was an excellent student. She made sure she never had to wear the dreaded "monitor"—a button worn by those who made the mistake of speaking the language they spoke at home instead of English, as the school demanded.

St. Cecilia was a very strict school. One day a student got into trouble for directly translating a phrase in Kikuyu to English in a letter to a friend. On the letter she said, "Here in St. Cecilia's we are fine, still eating fire." While the phrase actually meant "we are having a great time" in Kikuyu, the girl translated it incorrectly into English. Sister Christiana, one of the teachers at the school, read the letter and got very angry. She served the girl pieces of charcoal at mealtime so that she could eat the fire like she had said in her letter.

Even with the strict rules, nothing stopped Wangari from enjoying school life and doing well at the same time. Though some of the students owned shoes, they did not like to wear them much, so she and the other girls figured out a fun way to keep their feet clean before going to bed. After washing their feet, they carried one another to bed! The last person was the only one who wore shoes.

Wangari continued to excel at school, and went on to attend Loreto Girls High School near

Nairobi, the capital city of Kenya. She would spend her break time helping Mother Teresia, a science teacher at the high school, clean petri dishes and test tubes in the science lab. Slowly but surely, her teacher's friendship influenced Wangari's interest in science. Just like a growing tree, she wanted to stretch her mind. She did not want to become a nurse or a secretary like most girls she knew, but was far more excited about science.

Although she enjoyed school, Wangari

missed home: the green, slopy hills, the animals, gardens, food, friends, and relatives, and the stream that she had visited every day. She kept her connection with the land by working in the garden during holidays. As soon as she got home, she would make her way to the garden. Touching the soil felt good. She reached down to plant sweet potatoes, beans, maize, or millet. She helped weed and harvest. She had missed the land so much while at school that she would forget to stop working before dark.

She would make her way home in the dark by listening to the sound of flowing water and following the river. She counted the number of hills and observed the trees and thick vegetation that she knew so well to figure out where she was. She often stopped to gaze up the starry sky through the silhouette of the leaves. Oh, how beautiful it looked!

She could hear the crickets chirping, and every so often something rustled in the underbrush. She was not afraid. The animals belonged there just like she did. The beauty and cool evening helped her forget her tired body. When she got home, Wangari would stay outside gazing at the clear starry skies as she ate with the rest of her family.

When she was nineteen years old, Wangari finished high school, at which point she was considered highly educated in her village. Some people even thought she was too highly educated for a woman. While she was in school, neighbors and friends told her mother to not let her education continue. If some people were proud of her, they never told her that. In their culture, people did not give compliments in public, so that made sense, but Wangari was not waiting for compliments. She knew what she wanted to do. She wanted to learn more about science, wherever that took her.

When friends and teachers asked, "What if you do not pass your high school exam?" she would retort, "What do you mean? Of course I will pass." Wangari knew that determination and hard work would bring results.

Her goal was to attend Makerere University, the only university in East Africa at that time. But when the Joseph P. Kennedy Jr. Foundation opened up a scholarship program for Kenyan students to attend school in the United States, the Catholic bishop in Nairobi, who knew that Wangari had completed Loreto Girls High School at the top of her class, chose her as one of the students to go.

The scholarship allowed her free education first at Mount St. Scholastica College in Atchison,

Kansas, and then at the University of Pittsburgh in Pennsylvania. Studying in the United States was both fun and life-changing. In the Unites States, she saw how Black people were being mistreated by the policemen and others. She wondered why things like this were happening to Black people both back at home and in America, which was known as "the land of the free and home of the brave." She concluded that "education was part of the solution to many of the problems Black people were facing everywhere." By the end of her studies, like a tree, she had grown new branches and fruits. She learned to speak her mind without fear. She gained a willingness to listen, learn, think, and ask questions. She gained confidence. Little did she know that these were tools she was going to need back at home to fight for her people.

....

CHAPTER 4

Trees to the Rescue

Wangari came back to Kenya in 1966 with two degrees in biology. Being home felt liberating. She felt as free as all Kenyans, who had now been independent from British rule for three years. She was excited and could not wait to report for duty at her new job at the University College of Nairobi, a job she had been invited to fill.

However, this joyous homecoming quickly changed to disappointment. Even though she had been promised a job at the university, when she got there, the school administrators told her that the job was no longer hers. She was devastated. What was she going to do next? How was she going to survive? Wangari knew that she couldn't give up. She took a deep breath, lifted her head up, and determined that she was going to do whatever it took to succeed.

Several months later, Wangari got a different job at the University College of Nairobi and persevered through many difficulties. For example, the university did not want to provide women with a place to live or money to rent one, even though they gave male faculty those things. By doing that, the university was treating women worse than they treated men and saying that a woman was not as good as a man. This is called gender discrimination.

The university also used tribalism, the practice of favoring people from your own group over others, against Wangari: the professor who had hired her gave her first job to someone from his group, even though the person was still in Canada.

Wangari was determined to fight for equal rights for everyone. She and her friend Vertistine pushed back against the people at the university who weren't treating them fairly. Wangari had gotten married to a man named Mwangi in 1969, and as married women, Vertistine and Wangari were expected to benefit from their husbands' jobs. As professional women, though, they wanted to get benefits of their own, just like the men. They complained and talked to the university officials, but they were ignored. They decided to go to court, which would mean taking the head of the university, who was also the president of Kenya, through a whole legal process. Hoping to avoid that, the university gave up and gave them their rights. They were treated the same as male professors. Wangari learned that "sometimes you have to hold on to what you believe in because not everybody wishes you well or will give you what you deserve."

The university wasn't the only place where Wangari was treated differently, often worse, because of her gender. As time went on, she realized how often that happened. In 1971, she became the first woman in East and Central Africa to receive a doctoral degree. No matter how impressive that was, nobody said anything to celebrate this achievement, even though they did celebrate similar accomplishments when they were done by men. This did not stop her from going on to be the first woman to do many things, though, including becoming a senior lecturer in anatomy, the department chair of veterinary anatomy, and an associate professor, all at the University of Nairobi. And she did all of this while becoming a mother to three children as well.

When Wangari joined the National Council of Women of Kenya, NCWK for short, she found a place where rural women were encouraged to share their concerns. The women shared that they were no longer able to get wood to cook with and to fence their homes, food for their livestock, or water for cooking and drinking. They did not know what to do.

Wangari listened. Her Kikuyu culture and rural upbringing, as well as her scientific training, made it possible for her to find the source of the problem. Soil erosion was taking place because so many trees had been cut down. Coffee and tea plantations had replaced the trees, bushes, and grasses that protected the valuable soil and streams. The women now had to walk long distances to get fresh water and firewood.

How was she going to help them? Wangari thought long and hard.

"Plant trees!" she decided. It was a simple solution to a huge problem. *Everyone could easily plant trees*, she thought, *but I need to show them how.* She started showing people how to plant trees by doing

it at every opportunity she got. She wanted tree planting to have meaning. One such opportunity came on June 5, 1977, at the World Environment Day celebration at Nairobi's Kamukunji Park. Wangari and six other people planted seven trees. Each tree honored a community leader from a different ethnic group in Kenya. Wangari's hope was that, by planting the trees together, she could also encourage the people to come together and support each other and their new Kenyan democracy now that the British were gone. By planting trees with purpose, Wangari was determined to bring Kenyans together to promote democracy. And she was determined to fight for her rights and the rights of others, especially women, to show what it would take to make their democracy work. And it all came back to the trees.

....

CHAPTER 5

Tree Battles

Wangari knew that trees would provide firewood to cook with and material for fences and shelter. Not only that, but trees also released moisture into the air, promoting more rainfall and healthier streams and soil. She was confident that planting trees would heal the land.

Wangari believed in the harambee spirit, which means, "Let us all pull together." She knew that she could use that spirit to help people plant many trees, and she explained that saving the land could start with just one person. She said: "One person, one tree," and she knew that making a difference could be as simple as that. Every time she talked to one woman about planting a tree, she would ask them to tell another woman. Wangari did not only talk about it, though. She went all over the country planting trees herself and teaching small and large groups to do the same. If they

were able to plant crops, which so many of them were already doing, then they would be able to plant trees and help the land even more. Her work helping people plant trees meant that she had to leave her three children in the hands of a nanny or someone to care for them.

All over Kenya, people responded to her call. Wangari encouraged them to plant local fruit and medicinal trees. People planted trees such as: mubiru muiru for its berries, mukinduri for fire-wood, muheregendi for animal food, muthakwa wa athi to treat cattle, muluhakuha for timber. She became known as "Mama Miti"—the mother of trees. She encouraged women to plant "seedlings in rows of at least a thousand trees to form green 'belts' that would restore to the earth its cloth of green." The Green Belt Movement was born.

Mama Miti traveled from village to village, teaching people about trees. At the same time, she joined the movement against the oppressive and corrupt government of Daniel arap Moi, who was at that time the president of Kenya. Everywhere she went, Wangari encouraged the people she met to discuss their problems in their own words and language to find solutions that worked for them. Just as she used words to help people come together to plant trees, Wangari also used words to encourage people to be a part of their country's democratic process, by talking to each other and understanding the best path forward for them.

While Wangari and her Green Belt Movement were busy organizing and helping people, problems were continuing to brew in Kenya. Some people in the government did not want her to plant trees and improve the environment. They were angry when they realized that her teachings about freedom, peace and taking care of the environment, written in newspapers in Kenya and other countries, reached many people. These officials had made a lot of money by cutting and selling trees and land. They wanted to stop Wangari.

"Who is this woman who speaks with confidence?" they wondered. "Women are supposed to be quiet and let their husbands speak for them." Others said, "She is a bad example to women." And some other people said, "She is not following African culture by not listening to her husband; worse still, she is divorced. She should not talk at all." Of course, these comments made Wangari sad and she wondered what her three children felt. But as they grew older and watched and listened to what their mother was doing, she hoped they understood the good she was fighting for.

The government tried to block her work, but Wangari found a way around them. She organized people from Kenya and many other countries to visit Green Belt groups near Nairobi. They took the message of growing trees to their homes and countries. More people then grew more trees in more places.

Soon Wangari learned that the government was planning on building a sixty-story complex called the *Times* Complex, as well as a statue for President Moi, in Uhuru Park, right in the heart of the capital city. Where were people going to find beautiful green space to rest and get fresh air amid the noisy, crowded steel-and-pavement city? Wangari was not going to let the park be taken by the government.

In Kikuyu, the name Wangari means "she

who belongs to the leopard." Like a leopard, she and her friends fearlessly confronted the government. She wrote letters and sent copies to the media so that everyone knew about what was going on. The more she wrote, the more word spread.

She asked foreign investors and governments in the United States, the United Kingdom, and Germany to help stop the building of the *Times* Complex, explaining that it was a waste of money and bad for the environment.

Many people thought Wangari's efforts were doomed to fail. They wondered why Wangari kept on going. "Why don't you give up?" they asked her.

"Because after they are done with what is owned by the public, they'll come for what is mine and yours," she replied.

As a result of the efforts of Wangari and

her friends, the government gave in, and without warning, the fencing was removed, and that section of the park was open again. Wangari and her friends had succeeded! They went back to Uhuru Park and danced a dance of victory.

"I have seen time and again that if you stay with a challenge, if you are convinced that you are right to do so, and if you give it everything you have, it is amazing what can happen," Wangari said.

After that, Kenyans felt encouraged to speak against what they felt was not right. Wangari had led millions of people to move with confidence and courage. This was the confidence and courage they were going to need to grow enough trees to heal the land. Wangari never quit, and it is no wonder that one man told her: "You are the only man left standing."

....

CHAPTER 6

Growing Trees to Victory

Wangari's dream was to see a world of clear fresh water and trees growing undisturbed. She imagined women harvesting plenty of food, feeding their animals, drinking clean, fresh water, and collecting firewood from their own wood lots like she did as a little girl. These dreams encouraged her to move on when things got tough and to not give up. "What people see as fearlessness is really persistence," she said.

But even though she had achieved a great victory at Uhuru Park, the rocky days were not over yet. Wangari was arrested multiple times because the government did not want her to tell people that they were taking land meant for gardens, parks, and forests, and using it to build buildings. Whenever she was arrested, women and groups from all over the world would help get her out.

One time, while Wangari was recovering from an illness after being in jail for several days, some women came to ask if she would help them get their sons out of jail. They had been imprisoned for talking about freedom. Wangari decided to help them even though she was risking being arrested again herself.

Wangari and the women decided to have a hunger strike and prayer at Uhuru Park until

their sons were released from prison. They covered themselves with blankets to keep warm at
night. Friends brought water, juices, and glucose
to keep them healthy as they were fasting. They
sang freedom songs and hymns to keep their spir-
its up. Wangari and her friends named that part
of the park Freedom Corner, and it is still called
that to this day.

The women had been at the park for four days
when the police came to chase them away. When

they wouldn't leave, the police beat them. Many people were injured, including Wangari. While she was in the hospital, her friends gathered back together at nearby All Saints Cathedral. They stayed in the cathedral for a whole year, keeping up a vigil to bring attention to their cause. As soon as Wangari left the hospital, she joined them, and she stayed with them the entire rest of their time there. Finally, the government agreed to their demands and their sons were released. Once more, Wangari had led another group to succeed through perseverance.

In 1993, when different tribes started fighting over land, the government took sides and created even more conflict instead of working toward peaceful solutions. Mama Miti, however, used trees to help bring peace once again. She organized meetings for people to talk about their views and encouraged the planting of tree nurseries to share with people from other tribes, calling them "trees of peace."

By doing this, Wangari was helping, but she was also putting her own life in danger again, as powerful people wanted to stop her from bringing peace among the tribes. She made the decision to do her work in secret for fear of being arrested or killed. She moved under the cover of night. She dressed in clothes that would make it difficult for people to recognize her. She changed vehicles when traveling long distances. She changed residences often to avoid being discovered. She did all this to help bring peace during troubled times in Kenya.

Wangari knew that forests were like the lungs of the cities. The trees absorbed dirty air and gave clean air in return. So when she found out that Karura Forest had fallen into the hands of the government and was being given to a group of developers to build houses and golf courses, she sprang into action. In fact, the developers had started cutting down trees and were prepared to chase Wangari and her people away. But Wangari and her friends protested by planting trees and publishing information about the forest in the newspaper. Whenever the trees they had planted were uprooted, they would plant more. They went back to Karura Forest to take care of the tree nursery again and again until the developers gave up. Karura is now a thriving, beautiful forest with lots of animals, such as Sykes' monkeys, bushpigs, and hundreds of species of birds, and rare trees like the mihugu trees.

Wangari won many battles but she also lost some. Over twenty years, she was beaten and jailed numerous times. She knew that Kenya's democracy, which was supposed to give everyone in the country an equal voice in their government, had to continue growing like a tree in order to succeed. She pushed for better leadership for her country, and in 2002, she was elected as a member of parliament. In 2003, she was appointed as an assistant minister in the Ministry of Environment and Natural Resources. In that position, she could really be the Mama Miti she had always wanted to be. She could speak boldly for the people and the land without worrying who might come after her as a result.

In 2004, Wangari won the Nobel Peace Prize for her contribution to environmental development, democracy, women's rights, and peace. She

was the first African woman
to receive this honor. No
longer ignored, her extraor-
dinary work finally was
recognized.

Wangari received the
news with deep emotion.
She planted the Nandi flame
tree at her home in Nyeri, and
faced Mount Kenya weeping with joy. She wanted
the mountain to celebrate with her, but the mountain was covered with clouds. She wanted her
inspiration, Mount Kenya, to lift its clouds and
show its beautiful peak. She knew it was "proba-
bly weeping with joy, and hiding her tears behind
a veil of white clouds."

Winning the Nobel Peace Prize gave Wangari

many opportunities. She traveled and talked to people all over the world. She could now reach out through her new position like the migumo tree reaches out to the sky. In the same way, Mama Miti also reached out her hands to heal the land. She said: "The challenge is to restore the home of the tadpoles and give back to our children a world of beauty and wonder." The Green Belt Movement was invited to many countries to share what they were doing to protect the environment, and in 2006 they launched the Plant for the Planet: Billion Trees Campaign, with a goal of planting a billion trees by the end of 2007.

As a member of parliament, Wangari knew that the issues of human rights, women's rights, children's rights, taking care of resources, and peace formed the basis of what her work was all about. With this in mind, she agreed to become a goodwill ambassador to protect the Congo Basin forest, and she also became the presiding officer of the African Union's Economic, Social, and Cultural Council, where she helped raise up ideas of organizations to help people throughout the continent, including women, children, people with disabilities, artists, and more. Wangari also joined with other woman Nobel Peace Prize winners to address the causes of violence toward women.

After her death in 2011, her life was honored and recognized in many ways. The United Nations established the Wangari Maathai Forest Champion Award, which it started giving out in 2012. In that same year, Wangari Gardens was opened in Washington, DC. In 2013, Syracuse University in New York awarded her a doctor of science honorary degree, and the Wangari Maathai Trees and Garden was dedicated at the University of Pittsburgh. In 2014, a statue of her was unveiled at her former university in Atchison, Kansas. In 2016, Forest Road in Nairobi was renamed Wangari Maathai Road.

The Green Belt Movement expanded to have offices in Kenya, Washington, DC, and London. Even though Wangari is gone, the group still protects trees and raises funds to continue the work that she began. By the time Wangari passed away, the Green Belt Movement had planted over fifty-two million trees, and even more have been planted since.

Wangari Maathai persisted, and—no matter what your dream is—you should too.

HOW YOU CAN PERSIST

by Eucabeth Odhiambo

Wangari used her determination and bravery to bring change to many people and many places. To honor Wangari's bravery and work, here are some ideas:

1. Plant trees that grow locally where you live, and help others grow trees by showing them how easy it is.

2. Find ways to help the environment, and encourage people you know to learn how to take care of the environment too. Join together with others to form groups that work to improve the environment.

3. Continue with your work without worrying if other people aren't celebrating your achievements.

4. Use trees as gifts to make more friends and help the environment.

5. Encourage people with tree nurseries to sell trees that grow locally.

6. Find and share places where people can learn how to work together to solve the problems in their community.

Acknowledgments

I would like to express my appreciation to my family for their support and encouragement.

The following individuals deserve special thanks:

Rubin Pfeffer, who helped me put the facts in ways children could understand. Thanks for your guidance.

Talia Benamy and Jill Santopolo, whose guidance helped bring this book to what it is.

❦ References ❧

"Fight Against Development." Wangari Muta Maathai. ntu
.edu.sg/hp3203-2017-14/the-environment-and-government.

"Kenya: Wangari Maathai Attacked, 24 Jan 1999."
University of Pennsylvania—African Studies Center.
africa.upenn.edu/Urgent_Action/apic_12499.html.

Maathai, Wangari. "Nobel Lecture." Oslo, Norway,
December 2004. nobelprize.org/prizes/peace/2004
/maathai/26050-wangari-maathai-nobel-lecture-2004.

Maathai, Wangari. *Unbowed: A Memoir.* New York:
Anchor Books, 2007.

Napoli, Donna Jo, illustrated by Kadir Nelson. *Mama Miti:
Wangari Maathai and the Trees of Kenya.* New York:
Simon and Schuster, 2010.

New York Botanical Garden. *Tree Time: Mama Miti: Wangari Maathai and the Trees of Kenya.* (Read-aloud of *Mama Miti* by Donna Jo Napoli, illustrated by Kadir Nelson.)Video. February 26, 2021. youtube.com /watch?v=qw-4NC4vhr0.

Prévot, Franck, illustrated by Aurélia Fronty. *Wangari Maathai: The Woman Who Planted Millions of Trees.* Watertown, MA: Charlesbridge, 2015.

Rebel Girls, illustrated by Eugenia Mello. *Dr. Wangari Maathai Plants a Forest.* New York: Simon and Schuster, 2020.

Swanson, Jennifer. *Environmental Activist Wangari Maathai.* Minneapolis: Lerner Publishing Group, 2018.

"Wangari Maathai." Friends of Karura Forest. friendsofkarura.org/news-views/wangari-maathai.

"Wangari Maathai: Marching with Trees." *On Being with Krista Tippett.* April 6, 2006. onbeing.org /programs/wangari-maathai-marching-with-trees /#audio.

EUCABETH ODHIAMBO was born and raised in western Kenya. Her college studies focused on education and brought her to the US to attend Tennessee State University. She began her career as a classroom teacher and has taught all grades from kindergarten through middle school. Currently, she is a professor of teacher education at Shippensburg University. Eucabeth's first novel, *Auma's Long Run*, was published to great acclaim and was named a *Kirkus Reviews* Best Middle Grade Book of 2016 and a Children's Book Committee at Bank Street College Best Children's Book of the Year.

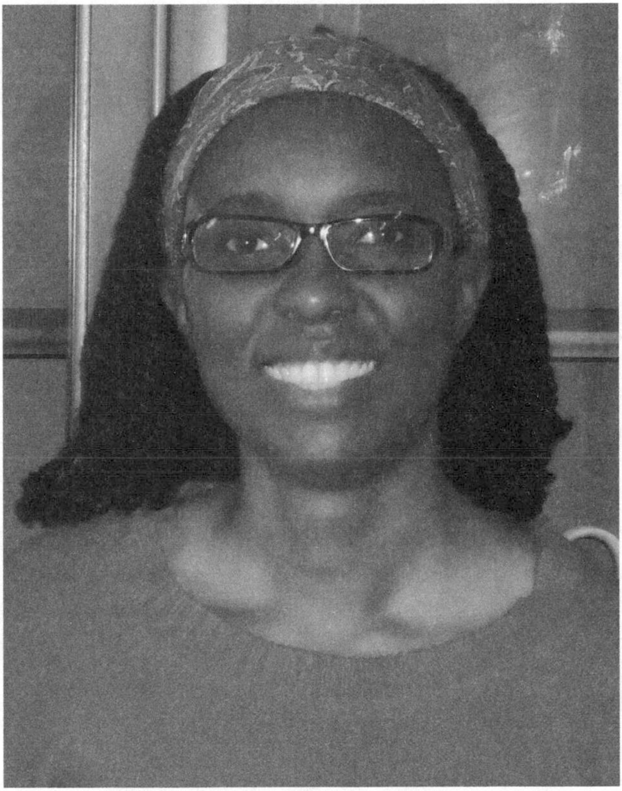

Courtesy of the author

GILLIAN FLINT has worked as a professional illustrator since earning an animation and illustration degree in 2003. Her work has since been published in the UK, USA and Australia. In her spare time, Gillian enjoys reading, spending time with her family and puttering about in the garden on sunny days. She lives in the northwest of England.

You can visit Gillian Flint online at
gillianflint.com
or follow her on Twitter
@GillianFlint
and on Instagram
@gillianflint_illustration

CHELSEA CLINTON is the author of the #1 *New York Times* bestseller *She Persisted: 13 American Women Who Changed the World*; *She Persisted Around the World: 13 Women Who Changed History*; *She Persisted in Sports: American Olympians Who Changed the Game*; *Don't Let Them Disappear: 12 Endangered Species Across the Globe*; *It's Your World: Get Informed, Get Inspired & Get Going!*; *Start Now!: You Can Make a Difference*; with Hillary Clinton, *Grandma's Gardens* and *Gutsy Women*; and, with Devi Sridhar, *Governing Global Health: Who Runs the World and Why?* She is also the Vice Chair of the Clinton Foundation, where she works on many initiatives, including those that help empower the next generation of leaders. She lives in New York City with her husband, Marc, their children and their dog, Soren.

You can follow Chelsea Clinton on Twitter
@ChelseaClinton
or on Facebook at
facebook.com/chelseaclinton

ALEXANDRA BOIGER has illustrated nearly twenty picture books, including the She Persisted books by Chelsea Clinton; the popular Tallulah series by Marilyn Singer; and the Max and Marla books, which she also wrote. Originally from Munich, Germany, she now lives outside of San Francisco, California, with her husband, Andrea, daughter, Vanessa, and two cats, Luiso and Winter.

You can visit Alexandra Boiger online at
alexandraboiger.com
or follow her on Instagram
@alexandra_boiger

Read about more inspiring women in the

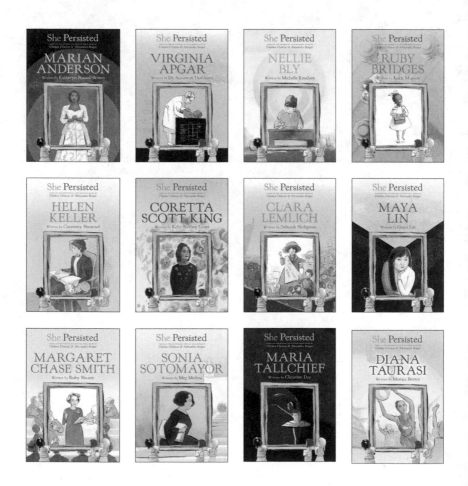

She Persisted series!

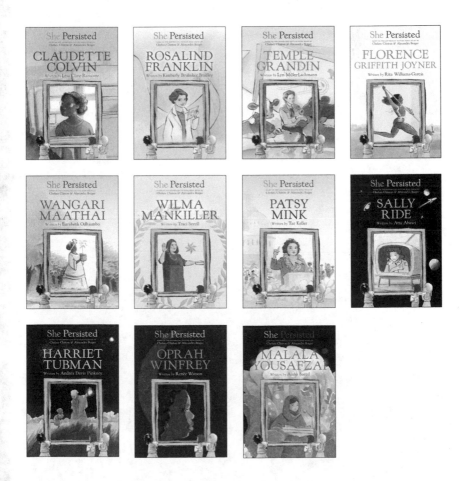